FOR ROBERT PENN WARREN

David R. Godine Publisher
Boston, Massachusetts

Copyright © 1974 by John Hollander

LCC 73-86336
ISBN 0-87923-084-3

Designed by Carol Shloss

Number 3 in the
FIRST GODINE POETRY
CHAPBOOK SERIES

Jan Schreiber, General Editor

The Head of the Bed

At the mountainous border of our two countries there is a village; it stands just below a pass, but some of the older houses lie higher up along the road, overlooking more of the valley than one might think. The border has never been heavily guarded, and our countries are peaceful. Theirs lies beyond the pass; in the other valley a large village looks up toward the mountains and toward us. The border itself is marked only by an occasional sign; but then there is the Trumpeter. His clear, triadic melodies break out through the frosty air, or through the swirling mists. From below, from above, the sound is commandingly clear, and it seems to divide the air as the border divides the land. It can be heard at no fixed intervals, and yet with a regularity which we accept, but cannot calculate. No one knows whether the Trumpeter is theirs or ours.

1

Heard through lids slammed down over darkened glass,
Trees shift in their tattered sheets, tossing in
Shallow sleep underneath the snoring wind.

A dream of forests far inside such sleep
As wakeful birds perched high in a dread wood,
Brooding over torn leaves, might mutter of

Rises over the pain of a snapped twig
That ebbs and throbs not with a shore rhythm
But with the pulsings of dark groves – as if

A bird of hurting swept over hooded
Places, fled, and at intervals returned –
Clocked by the broken aspirates roaring

Along their own wind, heard within their wood,
Their own deep wood, where, fluttering, first words
Emerge, wrapped in slowly unfolding leaves.

2

Where, where, where? Where is here? Where is Herr Haar,
Tendrils lashing across the light his eyes
Open on, Joker of Awakening?

Where is where? Where the cracked suddenness wide
On that frail wall, where amber filigree
As of an egg's marble vein his pillow;

Where webby vines clinging coldly to his
White eyeball fall away to dust; where hair
Hangs across the world, here is where. And there

Is the acknowledging skull of far wall –
Two hollow, shaded windows and a smudge
Of dark mirror between. And there is here

No light. Not yet. Deep in the woods' heart, soft,
Dim leaves close up again; heat lightning rips
Pallid sheets, silent, across roughened sky.

3

Floor lamps and their shadows warmed the room where
He lay dead in bed; and then the windows
Were thrown open to admit of the night.

Exhalations of buses rose hoarsely
Over the reservoir's onyx water
Beaded about with lights, an appalling

Brooch clutching the appalling shawl of the
Dark park through whose trees no relieving wind
Blew. No zephyr sniffed the window curtains

Pushing through the stuff of outer silence
That cars coughed in; only an old great-aunt
Waited, on her nightly visitation,

Denied again by his awakened, dark
Blood, as come bubbling up bone-gathering
Trumpetings of unscheduled, sombre cocks.

4

Slanting, lean, gray rain washing the palace
Steps floods the inner court: Vashti mutters
There, dripping among her ancillaries,

Of displeasure, loss, and now a cold walk
To distant parts of the palace, gutters
Roaring with possibilities, water

Burbling the Ballade of All the Dark Queens –
Not the wet abjects, but those who yet reign
(*Where is Lilith?*) in that they could refrain –

Not Hagar sent out among the dry rocks,
But Orpah opting for hers, and Martha
Answering her own hearth and electing

The bubbling merriment of her pudding,
Reading the night-girl Lilith's name in white,
Vanishing from her windy, drying sheets.

5

Coarse breath fanning the closed air by his ear
Stirred up the swarming night-bees who had been
Honeying nearby, where faces blossomed

Out of the darkness, where creepers mingled
With long, low-lying trunks, humming among
Damp hollows, herding and gathering there,

But unheard by him undreaming, by him
Beamed in upon by the wide moon who smeared
Light here and there into dark surfaces –

Madam Cataplasma, her anointment
Vast, her own outstretched form fantastic there
Beside him, as if on awakening

A filthy myth of Lilith would lie spilled
Like darkness on the sheet of light. He rolled
Out of this bad glade and slept darkly on.

6

He felt his hand feeling another hand
Feeling his own: staring up after a
Fly's noisiness, his bony image lay

Where he was beside himself, imbedded
In the nearby, the space readied and wide
And yawning, fed up with the emptiness

Of its tents, rags of cloudy percale hung
Over bumps and hummocks. It shaded them,
He and he lying and listening while

Kicked fabric fell softly over their bones.
Sighing settles: toward what does buzzing fly?
About what does the sound of breathing dream? –

An echo fleeing down twisted halls; a
Buzzing fly rising over him and his
Like something bland and vague deserting them.

7

Down the shaded street, toward an avenue
Of light, a gleaming picture receded:
The sudden lady, tall, fair and distant

Glided slowly, and her beautiful leg
Sole but unlonely, swung walking along
Between the companionable crutches,

Flesh hand in hand with sticks. He followed them
And waited in a sunny place, and when
She halted, there were woods. Turning her head,

She smiled a bad smile, framed by a shadow
Flung from a tower somewhere. He dared not move
Toward her one leg, toward her covered places

Lest he be lost at once, staring at where
Lay, bared in the hardened moonlight, a stump
Pearly and smooth, a tuft of forest grass.

8

The Hyperboreans gathered him up
And bore him across, out of the shadows,
Into their realm of tenderness where there

Is room enough, but where there are no gaps
Between the seeding and the gathering;
Nor wintering, in which recovering

Desire grows in its caves, nor the buzz
Of endless August, golden, deified:
No need for these. In that bland land he lay –

Envisioning frost and fallen silver,
Half hearing the cricket in the parching
Oat-straw, feeling tears from his weeping brow,

Dreaming of intervals lost – stretched out on
Wastes not of snow, nor sand, nor cloud, he tossed,
And knew not why, in that undying noon.

9

Leaving that unfair, seasonless land was
More than a traverse of uneasiness;
More than an antlike file over glacial

Sheets and then, at last, across the fold of
Pass, pausing above a final valley
Shining in a new light, and shivering

At the approach of strange, dark guards; more than
Their distrust, and their icy mustaches
Masking frowns at our tokens of passage

(He held a light bulb, heavy in his right
Pocket, and they, red stones in their left ones)
More than making one's way; and returning

Over a way not yet gone over, hurt
Like first smashings of light, shrunk to a lamp
Shaded, grim, sun-colored at four AM.

10

Beyond the cold, blue mountain and beyond
That, we shall wander on the pale hills when
Shadows give over bending along the

Slopes, and the silent midday light, unchanged
For hours and days, is pierced only by our
Two moving specks, only by the cricket's

Warm humming. Then, what we hear becoming
What we see, the gray; the wind enclosing;
The poplars' breath; the sad, waiting chambers.

Will there have been room? There will have been room
To come upon the end of summer where
Clustered, blue grapes hang in a shattered bell,

Or there, in a far, distant field, a swarm
Of bees in a helmet, metal yielding
Honey, balmy drops glistening on bronze.

11

Half his days he had passed in the shadow
Of the earth: not the cold, grassy shade cast
By a pale of cypresses, by pines spread

More softly across stony hilltops; not
Warm, gray veiling of sunlight that blotted
Up his own moving shadow on the ground;

But the dark cloak of substance beyond mass,
Though heavy, flung with diurnal panache
Over his heavier head, weighed it down.

Way down at the bottom of a shaft sunk
Through the grass of sleep to deep stone he lay,
Draped in the shade cast inward by the place

All outward shadows fall upon, and on
His tongue an emerald glittered, unseen,
A green stone colder in the mouth than glass.

12

When, as if late some night of festival
The skies open, do the insides of stars
Turn slowly out? At midnight, once, he finds

Himself looking up a familiar
Street and being shown a way of water:
Bordering the calm, unsubsided flood,

Gray frame houses with darkened roofs intact,
Minding the sky of paler gray; along
The surface of gray water, the tracing

Eye's anxious questions – only these have moved.
And save where – by a window giving on
His sunken yard – someone blind makes wordless

Music while his three graceless daughters wait
In the shadows for evening, all is gray
Silence, save for his resolved organ chords.

13

He awoke. Low in the sky in August
Blown clear by a cold wind, thinned-out clusters
Of distant stars whistling through darkness struck

Out at a momentary Jupiter
Passing at night, bright visitor, among
The passages of his twinkling bazaars.

And saw strung in the Scorpion a jewel
Of unmarred garnet, the old, the reddened
But not with shed blood, nor with ripening.

And saw and read by the diamonded Harp,
By crossbow Swan aimed along the pale stream
Southward, by all the miles of undialled light,

By the mark missed, by the unstinging tail,
The moment that was: the time of this dark
Light beyond, that seemed to be light above.

14

Grayish flakes like clay are falling as if
Of the sky falling at last on Chicken
Big, now grown huge and old, examining

The falling daylight from her crowded house,
The plausible, settled-for gray, dropping
Out of its cloudy, indeterminate

Swirl, its pale precipitate vanishing
At the full bottom of its fall, too light
To have swerved, too general to pile up,

These flakes of day, in a reaction
As if of flakes of, say, fictions taking
Place *in vitro*, trembling as the flask shakes –

In vivo then? behind this mottled glass
The awakener hears the greasy rain
Collapse on unglistening streets below.

15

The bright moon offends him: he plucks it out;
He opens all the seals of touch; he hears
The whirlwinds of his breathing; then it comes:

A last waking to a trumpet of light
From warm lamps turns him over gravely toward
Her long, bare figure, Lady Evening,

Who, while he lay unwaking, rearranged
Oddments of day on a dressing table,
Lowered gentle blinds, letting the night dawn,

And thought of their sole parting, the breaking
Of day; his journeys into day's mock night;
His sojourn with lilting Miss Noctae, witch

Of windless darknesses; his presiding
Eye, and his slowly unwinding heart;
Then lay beside him as the lamps burned on.

NEBUCHADNEZZAR'S DREAM

being a Commentary on *The Head of the Bed*
by John Hollander

Thy dream, and the visions of thy head upon thy bed, are these;
— DANIEL 2:28

Lilith, bride of Sammael as she became, nevertheless began as Adam's first wife. Perhaps she is due for some worship in these days of Liberation, and for all I know she currently may have her overt following, in one coven or another. But John Hollander is a traditionalist, and particularly in his nightmares. The *Zohar* tells us that, after being supplanted by Eve, Lilith 'flew to the cities of the sea coast,' thus explaining her manifestations to the poet in New York City. The demoness is immortal, and I would be surprised that so few poems have been devoted to her, except that I assume she is widely celebrated under the disguise of many names, not all of them mythological. Hollander names her only in the fourth and fifth sections of his dark sequence, but she lurks in or near every tercet of every part.

The 'two countries' of Hollander's prose prelude are life and the dream, and the Trumpeter of a prophecy belongs to both. At the poem's conclusion, the dreamer wakes 'to a trumpet of light' only to discover that the demarcations have become ghostlier, the sound keener, and the nightmare has been assimilated to life. Whether the poet is like the Nebuchadnezzar of the prophets Daniel and Blake, a Nebuchadnezzar who would not learn from the visions of the night, or hopefully more like the Nebuchadnezzar of Kierkegaard, who surmounted being a natural man, the close of this sequence does not tell us. In Babylon, early in the sixth century BC, Nebuchadnezzar II, the High King, set down the public prayer: 'May I attain eternal age.' The Hebrew prophets who

21

hated him gave him that age. It was Kierkegaard, following them, who gave the King of Babylon a true latecomer's chant, as the sufferer of seven transformations brooded obsessively on the Hebrew Lord, murmuring as refrain: 'No one knows where he dwells.' In so brooding, Kierkegaard's dreamer approached, not redemption, but the recognition of what was needful for redemption. Blake's Nebuchadnezzar, in his bestial crouch depicted on the last plate of *The Marriage of Heaven and Hell*, remains a less fanciful emblem of the relation of any natural selfhood to the world of its dream-work.

As I brood on *The Head of the Bed*, I am haunted by the truth Hollander begins to express as well as suffer: that the true muse of all poets necessarily afflicted with a sense of latecoming is Lilith. How does the tradition that speaks through Hollander's sequence call upon us to interpret her?

Begin with the assumption that the vision men call Lilith is formed primarily by their anxiety at what they perceive to be the beauty of a woman's body, a beauty they believe to be, at once, far greater and far less than their own. Lilith becomes the threat to male narcissism, and so the true muse, not the false idealization of a muse that crowds through poetic history. For what is the function of a muse? To make the poet remember. But what has he forgotten? That he is, as the Emersonian poet Christopher Cranch wrote, only a column left alone of a temple once complete. Lilith, 'body's beauty' as Rossetti called her, reminds the poet that he is bound to origins and not to ends, that his autonomy is (at best) a saving fiction.

Hollander's triadic melodies, unlike the Trumpeter's, are knowingly unclear, and break out only through the swirling mists of the Fuseli-like phantasmagoria of nightmare that rides with her ninefold of anxieties all through this Kabbalistic sequence. The mythic world giving context to *The Head of the Bed* is the over-determined

22

thicket of meanings that made up the theosophical universe of the Great Rabbi, Isaac Luria, Lion of Safed, and of the copious redactor, Moses de Leon, who compiled the *Zohar*.

Kabbalah, in its root, is another word meaning tradition, that which was not only given but was joyously received. Always in Kabbalistic literature what moves and repels me are the stigmata of a psychology of latecoming. No latecomer is capable of explaining that which forever possesses priority over him, and no latecomer is capable of wholly fresh creation. The Kabbalistic interpreter is neither an explainer nor a poet; he is necessarily a revisionist. And this must be his working principle (which I render from the *Zohar* III, 152a):

As wine in a jar, if it is to keep, so is the Torah, contained within the outer garment. Such a garment is constituted of many stories; but we, we are required to pierce the garment.

The Head of the Bed, however Hollander came to it, is a Kabbalistic text, haunted by an implicit psychology of belatedness. As its interpreter, I swerve from it, strive to complete it antithetically, empty myself out in relation to its self-emptying, raise myself to a Sublime that will counter its afflatus, purge myself as it purges itself into solitude, and seek finally to make it return from its death in the colors as much my own as any of Hollander's. Wilde, visionary critic who greatly deplored the Decay of Lying, would bless my quest to see this text as in itself it really is not, which is to say, as to me truly it is. For the sequence is Hollander's version of a Nebuchadnezzar's dream, and I come to it as its Daniel.

The dreamer in canto I creates his images out of rhymes and consonances, a process sporadic but incessant throughout the sequence. *Heard, wind, birds, perched, wood, bird, hurting, words;* the movement indeed is from 'broken aspirates' to 'where, fluttering, first words/Emerge,' according to a dream-equation: *words = birds*. What the

23

sleeper dreams is the poet's origins *qua* poet, the primal
scene of Poetic Incarnation being here not the Whit-
manian 'ebbs and throbs . . . with a shore rhythm' near
a maternal ocean, but the 'pulsing of dark groves,' a
sacred wood paternal and sacrificial. When, at the start
of canto 2, the sleeper is awakened prematurely by his
own hair, 'Herr Haar,' he confronts an ancestral skull in
the night-wall, and again we overhear a faint, unmistak-
able Oedipal guilt. In canto 3 the sleeper associates the
New York night with the memory of a watchful crone
out of childhood, forerunner of darker mysteries, as these
three introductory cantos close.

With the dense, Pre-Raphaelite canto 4, the sequence
proper begins. Though the influence of Rossetti is direct
(his version of Villon, and his 'Body's Beauty' from *The
House of Life*), the verbal style is precisely that of the
American Pre-Raphaelitism of Trumbull Stickney and
Conrad Aiken:

> *Now in the palace gardens warm with age,*
> *On lawn and flower-bed this afternoon*
> *The thin November-coloured foliage*
> *Just as last year unfastens lilting down.*
> (STICKNEY, *Eride*, v)

> *And in the hanging gardens there is rain*
> *From midnight until one, striking the leaves*
> *And bells of flowers, and stroking bales of planes*
> *And drawing slow arpeggios over pools.*
> (AIKEN, 'And in the Hanging Gardens')

Hollander's erotic dream studies the nostalgias with an
American belatedness, identifying the poet with sad
Biblical heroines of rejection and exile, yet distinguishing
between the passive outcasts and the self-reliant (Orpah
and Martha, in preference to Vashti and Hagar; see the
second poem, 'Orpah Returns to Her People,' in

24

Hollander's first book of poems, *A Crackling of Thorns*, 1958). This distinction vanishes with the enthrallment to Lilith, a night-girl about whom we cannot learn too much. As the Adversary Female of Kabbalah, she presides over many visionary fantasies, but they can be fitted to a single pattern: she is the muse of self-gratification, of dark secret love, of Narcissus encountering himself in the vegetable glass of nature. Mother of imps, Lilith is a perpetually self-replenishing demoness, and truly the eternal goddess of all latecomers. For Hollander, descendant of the Kabbalistic Rabbi Loew of Prague, she is, remarkably, a being of light, and a vegetation goddess, in a scene that seems drawn by Blake's disciple, Edward Calvert. Compare his remarkable wood engraving, 'The Ploughman' (*Victoria and Albert Museum*) to this:

> ... *where faces blossomed*
>
> *Out of the darkness, where creepers mingled*
> *With long, low-lying trunks, humming among*
> *Damp hollows, herding and gathering there,*
>
> *But unheard by him undreaming* ...

Hollander's vision also is of a secondary paradise, but for so guilty a sensibility every paradise belongs to Lilith, or to her surrogate, 'Madam Cataplasma, her anointment/Vast,' whose name means 'poultice' (see Tourneur's *The Revenger's Tragedy*). Lilith's origins are properly hidden in mythology, but the name seems vaguely Sumerian, and most Midrashic tradition insists on her priority over our mother Eve. Hollander speaks of 'a filthy myth of Lilith,' filling the mouth with almost too much luxury of sound, because of the tradition that God formed Lilith neither from pure red clay and dust, like Adam, nor from Adam's rib, like Eve, but from sediment and various filth.
Tradition holds also that Lilith abandoned Adam be-

25

cause of a quarrel over sexual dominance, particularly related to the problem of position in intercourse, with Adam insisting upon the missionary posture, and Lilith refusing to lie beneath him, as she would not yield priority to clay over sediment, dust over filth. If Lilith's name *was* of Hebrew origin, presumably it derived from the word for 'night' (hence Hollander's 'night-girl'), but more likely she began as a Babylonian wind-demon (hence the 'coarse breath fanning the closed air' in Hollander's fifth canto). For nearly all subsequent tradition, our filthy myths of Lilith stem from the *Zohar*, where she is the female of the Leviathan, and many other dark manifestations. But this is her central epiphany, which I translate from *Zohar, Vayikra*, 19a:

In the Great Abyss, down in the depth, there is that spirit called Lilith, a hot and burning female, who first had intercourse with Adam. When Adam was created and his body finished, the spirits of the Left Side, a thousand in number, congregated around the completed body, each one attempting to penetrate it, until finally God drove them away by a descending cloud, that came down when God said: 'Let the earth bring forth the living creature' [Genesis 1:24]. Then it brought forth a spirit to breathe into Adam, who thus became complete, with two sides, as it says: 'And God breathed into his nostrils the breath of life; and man became a living soul' [Genesis 2:7]. When Adam arose, Eve was fixed to his side, and the Holy Spirit spread in him to each side, and so perfected itself. Afterwards, God sawed Adam in two and fashioned Eve, and brought her to him as a bride is brought to the canopy. When Lilith saw this, she fled to the cities of the sea coast, where she is still, attempting to catch men in her snares. Only when the Almighty destroys wicked Rome, will He then settle Lilith among its ruins, for she is the ruin of the world, as it is written: 'Yea, the night-hag shall repose there, and shall find her a place of rest' [Isaiah 34-14, where the word *lilith* is used for the only time in the text of the Hebrew Bible].

As the *Zohar* goes on to note, Lilith flees Adam when the *neshamah* or soul is placed in him. She has not fled many poets since, and rather seems to have the power of driving their souls from them, as she does to Hollander when he emulates the dying Hadrian in a dream of death at the close of canto 6, 'like something bland and vague deserting them.'

The vision of a saving 'sudden lady, tall, fair and distant,' rises in canto 7, but Hollander's version of the *Shekhinah* is not the Kabbalistic 'beautiful woman without eyes' but a cripple more out of the European Decadence, one-legged and on crutches. This displacement of Geza Roheim's mythological 'woman with a penis,' Aphrodite as phallic girl, is an equivocal emblem anywhere, but particularly negative in a Kabbalistic context, where it ends as the obsessive Narcissistic revelation of the closing lines of canto 7. Recoiling from this horrified nadir of vision, the poet begins a triad of cantos that will culminate in the relative serenity of canto 10, the turning-place of the sequence, where nightmare at last begins to be vanquished by peace.

Cantos 8–10 rely upon the myth of the Hyperboreans, dwellers 'beyond the mountains' and 'beyond the North wind,' whose earthly paradise in the far North was sacred to Apollo. In Hollander's dream-allegory, the Hyperboreans represent simply his escape route from the world of Lilith into the world of peace, a route identical with the process of becoming a poet, and echoing many poets and poems. Canto 8 echoes, sometimes deliberately, Spenser's Gardens of Adonis, Lovelace's 'The Grasshopper,' Tuckerman's 'The Cricket,' Stevens' 'A Discovery of Thought,' and Hart Crane's 'The Broken Tower.' In the next canto, other sources of vision are invoked, including the older version of the film *Lost Horizon* and the Hemingway story 'The Snows of Kilimanjaro,' to help suggest a menacing rite-of-passage between realms of being. The beautiful canto 10, with its traditional emblems of achieved poetic peace, echoes Stevens' characteristic mode of resolution:

> *There will have been room*
> *To come upon the end of summer where*
> *Clustered, blue grapes hang in a shattered bell.*

With the modulation into the final third of his sequence, the poet begins to pass judgment upon himself. The opening of Canto 11 deliberately echoes a great passage of Sir Thomas Browne, from his *Notebooks:*

Half our days we pass in the shadow of the earth; and the brother of death exacteth a third part of our lives. A good part of our sleep is peered out with visions and fantastical objects, wherein we are confessedly deceived. The day supplieth us with truths; the night with fictions and falsehoods.

For these unsaving fictions and falsehoods, the poet chastises himself, echoing the Rossetti translation of Dante's stony sestina, *To the Dim Light and the Large Circle of Shade.* The greatest of precursors, Milton, is invoked in the following canto, which relies upon the legend attached to the Jewish festival of Simchas Torah, that the skies open in response to the congregants' rejoicing in the Law. With canto 13, something closer to self-acceptance is achieved. Lilith's body, which terminated in a serpent's tail, is transformed into the constellation Scorpio, the poet's birth-sign, with its 'unstinging tail.' This canto attempts a sky-scape, on the model of Stevens' *Auroras of Autumn*, with Jupiter passing at night like the Haroun Al-Rashid of Tennyson's beautiful early poem. The Orphic lyre appears as 'the diamond Harp,/By crossbow Swan,' identified with Orpheus as archetypal poet. 'The pale stream' of the Milky Way illuminates a lost epiphany, 'the moment that was' hinting at a kind of deferred Gnostic salvation: 'the time of this dark/Light beyond, that seemed to be light above.'

As the snow descends in the pre-dawn gloom of canto 14, transcending the grotesque enlargements of children's stories (Chicken Little 'now grown huge and old') the sleeper finally wakens, uncertain whether the snow itself is a visionary experience ('fictions taking/Place *in vitro*'), a Lucretian swerving of particles in a flask or test tube, or an actual precipitate in the animal body, *in vivo*, in a greasy rain collapsing on streets incapable of further givings-back of the light. The final canto juxtaposes Lady Evening, a realized apocalypse or actual *Shekhinah*, to the final appearance of Lilith as 'lilting Miss Noctae, witch/ Of windless darknesses.' Images of a Last Judgment – the plucking out of the Romantic moon as presiding but offending Eye, the seals, whirlwinds, a last trumpet of light – herald a clarification that the poem's final tercet lacks the revelation to assert for itself. The poet has dreamed Nebuchadnezzar's dream, and at the close of the cycle knows that he tells us implicitly he must dream it over and over again.

Following Wilde, we turn to the Highest Criticism, our own version of this Nebuchadnezzar's dream, the filthy myths of our own visions of Lilith. In Heraclitus, Death is Earth, Sleep is Water, Waking is Air. Fragment 77 reads:

Man kindles a light for himself in the night-time, when he has died but is alive. The sleeper, whose vision has been put out, lights up from the dead; he that is awake lights up from the sleeping.

Take this as motto, and by its light read Lilith for what she is and must be, a myth of Earth masking as Water and Air. Kabbalists and Gnostics, like latecomer poets, confound Lilith with the Muse of Nihilism, the Lower Sophia, who must suffer grief, fear, bewilderment, and ignorance, the 'affections' of all strong sensibilities

29

afflicted by a psychology of belatedness. The fifth 'affection' in the Valentinian Speculation, most poetic of all Gnosticisms, was the 'turning back,' a conversion towards the lost Light. *The Head of the Bed* nears greatness as a Kabbalist and Gnostic text by its authentic and vivid portrayal of the four dark 'affections' and its poignant approach to the fifth 'affection' of a 'turning back.'

The Gnostic Lower Sophia is akin to the Kabbalistic metaphor of the *Shekhinah*-in-exile. But even the *Shekhinah* still-at-home, within *En Soph*, the Infinite Godhood, possesses an ambivalence unknown in the unfallen Higher Sophia within the Valentinian Pleroma or original Fullness. Hollander's version of the *Shekhinah*, the 'Lady Evening' of his final canto, is not wholly distinguishable from the last appearance of his Lilith, 'lilting Miss Noctae,' since they never exist simultaneously, but only in continuity with one another. Each has her terrible aspect, as in Kabbalah, where the *Shekhinah* stands as much for the divine power of 'stern judgment' as for the divine quality of 'mercy.' To cite the *Zohar* again: 'Sometimes the *Shekhinah* tastes the other side, the bitter side, and then her countenance is darkened.'

Filthy myths of Lilith actually are filthy myths of the male dread of female otherness, and of what the male envies as female proximity to origins. Primal scenes, for poets, are less the scenes where they were begotten than those where they were instructed. Every poet, as he aspires towards strength, wants to be the universe, to be the whole of which all those others are parts:

> *And all the world lies well before you*
> *And in denial you glimpse the truth*
> *Whose recognition will restore you*
> *To the cool savagery of youth.*
> (JAN SCHREIBER, 'Camelot')

No poet, alas, can be so restored. Hollander's sequence,

like all his work, is incurably elegiac, and in that quality possesses a peculiar *clinamen*, a swerve or twist away from British and European study of the nostalgias, that has distinguished American poetry at least since the Age of Emerson. American psychopoetics are dominated by an American difference from European patterns of the imagination's struggle with its own origins. The literary psychology of America is necessarily a psychology of belatedness, in which the characteristic anxiety is not so much an expectation of being flooded by poetic ancestors, as already *having been* flooded before one could even begin. Emerson's insistence upon Self-Reliance made Whitman and Dickinson and Thoreau possible, and doubtless benefited Hawthorne and Melville despite themselves. But the Scene of Instruction that Emerson sought to void glows with a more and more vivid intensity for contemporary American poets, who enter upon a legacy that paradoxically has accumulated wealth while continuing to insist that it has remained poverty-stricken.

Piaget, in studying the child's cognitive development, has posited a dynamic in which the egocentric infant develops by a progressive decentering until (usually in adolescence) the decentering is complete. The child's space then yields to universal space, and the child's time to history. Having assimilated much of the Not-Me, the child at last accommodates his vision to the vision of others. Poets, we can assume, are children who have *assimilated* more than the rest of us, and yet somehow have *accommodated* less, and so have won through the crisis of adolescence without totally decentering. Faced by the primal scene of Instruction, even in its poetic variant (where the Idea of poetry first came to them), they managed to achieve a curious detachment towards crisis that made them capable of a greater attachment to their own wavering centers. In American poets, I surmise, the detachment must be more extreme, and the consequent

31

resistance to decentering greater, for American poets are the most conscious latecomers in the history of poetry. All men are belated in their stance towards all women. All Kabbalists and Gnostics are latecomers in their stance towards divinity. Combine the Gnostic or Kabbalistic temperament with a male American desperately intelligent about his own origins, and you get a series of latecomer bards from the Melville of *Timoleon* through the Crane of *The Bridge* on to a large group of greatly talented and greatly handicapped contemporary Americans. Hollander's remarkable achievement is to have so dreamed his own nightmares as to have joined, if not quite the universal, at least the national predicament of our poetry. Seven times passed over Nebuchadnezzar, and did not suffice to save him. No contemporary Nebuchadnezzar can dream to save himself, or us. It is enough to take from the dream-work of Instruction a style fit for our despair.

HAROLD BLOOM